INTERCITY 225

LEEDS TO LONDON

A Traveller's Book

Maureen Ellis

Helpston Signal Box

First published in 1993 by Hawksheath Press, 11 Main Street, Shadwell, Leeds, LS17 8EU (with help from the Yorkshire Art Circus, School Lane, Glasshoughton, Castleford, WF10 4QH)

Printed by: F M Repro Ltd, Repro House, 69 Lumb Lane, Roberttown, Liversedge, West Yorkshire, WF15 7NB

Typesetting: Pam Davenport

Photographs: the author

Cover Design:Brian Lewis and the author

ISBN 0 9522463 0 9

CONTENTS

125/225: Maps, Men and Mulberries

Cross Gates: Lighthouses, Lodges and Lamps

Leeds: Rhubarb, Russians and River Aire

Wakefield: Wars, Wanderings and Waterton

Doncaster: Engineers, Engines and the Eaa

Retford: Cannons, Canals and Cafés

Newark: Printers, Peers and Parliamentarians

Grantham: Mathematics, Manors and Mermaid Bones

Peterborough: Poets, Psychiatry and Publishers

Huntingdon: Daffodils, Decapitations and Diaries

St Neots: Postmen, Priories and Paper

Sandy: Owls, Ornithology and Oystercatchers

Biggleswade: Pears, Pilots and Puddings

Hitchin: Henry VIII, Horses and Hiz

Stevenage: Bowls, Brouhahas and Burial Mounds

Welwyn Garden City: Viaducts, and Victorias and Valleys

Hatfield: Lies, Larchs and Lords

Potters Bar: Gates, Graves and Germans

Hadley Wood and Barnet: Feuds, Friendships and Fighting

Alexander Palace and Finsbury Park:

Fireworks, Fires and Foreigners

London Kings Cross: Facades, Fish and Funerals

125/225: Man, Maps and Mulberries

The Intercity train from Leeds to London is full of the restless; the contented are at home in their beds at 7am or waking up to the reassuring thought of another day similar to the previous one. In the 1980s the restless were all talking of the 125s, the High Speed Trains that ran hourly to the capital from most major cities. British Rail's development of the HSTs was proving a tremendous boost to its image, even if it was only an interim measure to the development of the 225s.

Each month, bursting with self-importance, I took my place in the 125 to attend this meeting or that, or even to go to a theatre performance and return on the sleeper. Around me were success stories and students; later in the day relations were reuniting and shoppers going shopping.

People on the train never lost their interest for me; there was youth pouring over textbooks, people with tickets for New Zealand and African men and their families in flowing robes returning to their native lands. There were Asian families creating a two hour microcosm of Bombay as they ate spiced food and yoghurt; quiet Americans retracing ancestral paths and exhausted Czechoslovakians en route from the east. The first class passengers were more uniformly suited but there would be the twist of a purple silk tassel over a QC's document and the familiar face of an MP.

The travel itself was exciting as the train hurtled through green fields, over rushing rivers and held up cars on country lanes at level crossings. From the high vantage point could be seen pylons, giant robots marching towards their power stations; waste land of wetland encroaching towards the tracks; and the train passed through stations with historic names.

4

On one journey approaching Peterborough from the North the train passed the signal box at Helpstone and I recognised the birthplace of John Clare, poet and wanderer. With the connection of those two facts, the signal box and the poet, came the whole impact of the variety of associations of the places through which the train was passing. The journey was no longer from A to B, it was from A through a conglomeration of interests eventually to B, and later some of the places on the way to London became my goal for their own sakes.

Every roamer needs a map and I needed several. The one inch to one mile Ordnance Survey maps provided a dazzling array of facts and could in themselves provide complete armchair travel. The engineering feat of the nineteenth century in pushing a track northwards through cuttings and over roads and rivers is there in picture form for mile after mile. What a hill obscures from the view of the traveller, the Ordnance Survey map gives him a periscope to view. It also names every nook and cranny of countryside surrounding the railway.

The climate changes in the two hundred miles from north to south and with it the vegetation. Windswept Yorkshire gives way to beechy Midlands and the more sultry south. But man has always challenged nature and grown what he will against all odds and Leeds folk are no exception. As if defying latitude, two proud mulberry trees flourish outside The Faversham pub near the university and disgorge ripe red fruit each year.

Feet in the soil and head in heaven, monks have been responsible for introducing many non-indiginous plants such as liquorice in Pontefract and vines in Leeds. Over the fenlands from Peterborough the sweet smell of strawberries wafts and at Kew Gardens the flora of seven continents is captured by grace of plant hunters such as Tradescant and Sir Joseph Banks.

The 225 may be a small adventure for the traveller but if he has his head firmly in his papers and his goal set on London he will miss many of the interim connections. Not just railway links to Hull and Scunthorpe, March and Cambridge but links between people and places; places and people and their assorted wanderings. The following chapters will follow this theme.

I wish to thank Richard for his continuing interest in this book; Veronica Kelly for her illustrations, George Capel and Martin Stray of Harrogate Reference Library; Gordon Watson, Senior Keeper of Wakefield Museum, and David Thompson, Public Relations Officer of British Rail.

Tourist Information staff have consistently been helpful when I was searching for an initial point of interest. The Yorkshire Art Circus staff - especially Pam Davenport, my minder, and Brian Lewis - have kept me going to the point of completion of this book.

Maureen Ellis
June 1993

John Smeaton

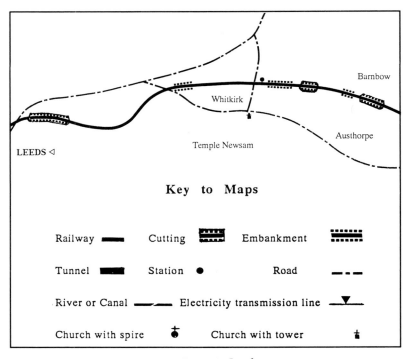

Barnbow

Whitkirk

Austhorpe

Temple Newsam

LEEDS ◁

Key to Maps

Railway	▬	Cutting	🔲	Embankment	▦
Tunnel	▬	Station	●	Road	– ▬ –
River or Canal	▬▬	Electricity transmission line			▼
Church with spire	⚲	Church with tower			⚲

Cross Gates to Leeds

Cross Gates: Lighthouses, Hedges and Lamps

Journeys have to start somewhere even if in the recesses of the mind and this one began each time at Cross Gates railway station. It is a station of concrete, a nonentity, hardly marked by anything but an oblong sign on the straight bit of line from York to Leeds. However it is not quite of the 1990s; there is still a manned ticket office. There are people in Cross Gates who still remember the pre-Beeching era and the Victorian station with six cast iron pillars supporting the glass roof. There were Ladies and Gents Waiting Rooms on either side of the track, the privet hedges were trimmed like soldiers' Busbys and the bridge leading to the town was lit by gas lamps until 1972. In the early days the train was the only means of public transport to Leeds, Wetherby and Castleford.

In the heyday of Yorkshire Mining, men used the busy branch line to Castleford and Kippax. During the war female workers at Thorp Arch Munitions Factory travelled to and from work, warming themselves in waiting rooms still heated by coal fires. In the days prior to the 1940s, the station and track hummed with manpower. There were five signal boxes, three for Cross Gates and two for Killingbeck. Each section had its men, a goods yard foreman and porter, a ticket collector and porter on each shift, and a chief clerk and under clerk who covered both shifts. The railway workers lived in 1-5 Station Cottages; the teams of four gangers each responsible for maintenance of a section of railway track; the plate layers and signal and telegraph line men.

The end of the war bought an end to all this and in the 1950s the Thorp Arch Workers Special ceased. The forlorness of the

Lighthouse Monument to John Smeaton in Whitkirk Church

10

war gave way to another kind of emptiness; the ripping up of the branch line to Wetherby and Thorp Arch and degration of Victorian splendour to concrete bunker. The temptations of the Ritz Cinema at the end of the railway bridge and the Regal Cinema were taken over by the television age. In 1967 the railway cottages were sold to private owners and in 1969 the signal box was demolished.

Running out of Cross Gates centre eastwards is Austhorpe Lane which leads down to the delightful Austhorpe Hall, a 1664 building, then it is out into the flat countryside of Yorkshire with its potatoes and rhubarb.

Engineers are the traveller's friend. They put dreams into reality; give man wings and take him on a safe way. The early engineers of the railways were often men who stayed in their native towns such as Doncaster and developed the sophistication of our present day system.

Tiny Austhorpe cradled a giant not of the iron network but of lighthouses, John Smeaton. He was born at Austhorpe Lodge, demolished in 1926, which was on the present site of Austhorpe Primary School. Smeaton was born in 1724 and was educated at Leeds Free Grammar School; at first studying law to please his father, he later turned to mechanics. In 1752 he was requested to undertake the rebuilding of the lighthouse on the Eddystone reef, off the coast of Plymouth. Although it was soon replaced by a fourth lighthouse, it remains famous because the top portion was re-erected on Plymouth Ho; the stump can still be seen at sea. Another of his lighthouses stood at Spurn Point, Yorkshire. Smeaton died aged 68 years back in Austhorpe Lodge. A plaque commemorates him in Whitkirk Church and Leeds Education Department paid their tribute by naming a school and sports centre after him.

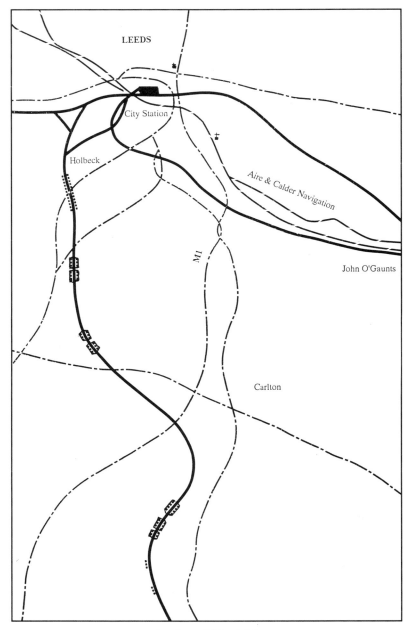

LEEDS

City Station

Holbeck

Aire & Calder Navigation

M1

John O'Gaunts

Carlton

Leeds to Wakefield

Leeds: Rhubarb, Russians and the River Aire

As befits a city of commerce, Leeds sits astride rail, road and river.
The great canal from Liverpool to Leeds talks of transport. Today
in Granary Wharf different sorts of trade are conducted -
decorated birthday cakes and patchwork, the creative harshness
of modern sculpture takes shape and some Oxfam volunteers
explain the iniquities of South Africa.

The 225 usually leaves from Platform 5, a workshop on
wheels; a mobile restaurant; movement for the restless. For two
or three hours the traveller creates his permanency round a table
and he looks out of the window. The track goes through historic
Holbeck where courtyards of Victorian workshops retain the
robustness of industry. There is Sawmill Street off Water Lane
where original use has given way to modern matters; the motor
car is catered for in a repair shop and Crossley Metal Finishing
burnish brass and copper objects. It is no messing here, hard
work and human grease are the currency, and cobbles here give
way to tarmac.

Then the train is out of the city and into the fields. A cousin
of mine recounted that at the beginning of his journey northwards
he had been told by his father that he would recognize Yorkshire
by its coal mines and rhubarb fields. 'There are coal miners and
rhubarb growers and nobody else,' said my uncle. Although an
exaggeration, the soil between Leeds and Wakefield is ideal for
rhubarb's growth. Its history is a long one. Ancient man was
troubled by constipation. In 2700 BC the Chinese recommended
the roots of rhubarb as a laxative and the Greeks imported dried
root from there and southern Russia both as a laxative and as a
remedy for stomach and chest pains. Venereal disease has always
outstripped its cures and the sixteenth century, that age of

13

nautical discovery and foreign trade, was no exception. Rhubarb was its penicillin. But a mistake had been made; the wrong species had been imported and was useless as a medicinal herb. Rheum rhabarbarum, known as bastard rhubarb, was used sparingly as a pot herb as it caused violent gut contractions. Eventually the correct medicinal species was imported from Russia in 1762 and the powdered root supplied to hospitals. Placebo or powder keg the roots could also be used as a red dye.

Roots and leaves had been tried, now it was the turn of forced stems to hit the market and it was the lucky mistake of the original importation of the wrong species that proved so fortunate for Yorkshire, as it was this non-medicinal species that had culinary value. The discovery that the leaf stalks were delicious probably came from that most food conscious of countries, France; they made a honey sweetened rhubarb marmalade.

The red stems started a craze amongst the Chelsea set and aristocracy for use as a pudding. By 1815 it was growing in the Chelsea Physic Garden and in 1870 it came to Yorkshire. Ask around Rothwell and Carlton and they will tell you about the low dark forcing huts of Oldroyd's, Dobson's or Crossley's. Pre-chilled crowns are brought into candle lit huts where the heat forces them prematurely into growth. The growth of this miniature forest is not silent, each shining crown exploding with a pop to extrude lime green leaves aloft its trunk of red. Mrs Oldroyd of Ashfield House, Carlton showed me one of the sheds. She shone a torch into the darkness and a technicolour miniature forest sprang into view. Exclusion of light forces the stems upwards and maintains their appetising pinkness. Today they are picked, packed and parcelled to all directions of the country. One main attraction is that it is the first of the home produced pie fillers.

The fields between Leeds and Wakefield that my uncle talks of are, in the summer, a forest of green umbrellas and mature red stalks ready for picking. Their spectacular display is not yet at an end, for if left to seed a ten foot stalk will shoot up bearing racemes of flat seeds. The Chelsea set now display these in carboys as dried flowers. The scientific quest for new and improved varieties continues and remains firmly based in the north. Plant hunting and reliance on imports of the right species is no longer necessary; the journey goes on in the laboratory and in glass houses.

Commercial growers have access to advice from Stockbridge House at Cawood, Selby, where new varieties are bred with names like Stockbridge Harbinger and Cawood Delight. The latter has a deep red colour which is not lost in cooking and freezes well. Scientific work examines spacing for better yields, shorter sticks for ease of packing and virus-free pot grown varieties. The Northern Horticultural Society at Harlow Carr Gardens, Harrogate lodges the national collection with at least seventy cultivars.

Now attention is back to the railway track and the Ordnance Survey map and the recollection that plans for a high speed train from Leeds to London were afoot in 1959 to be frozen by Ernest Marples but actually begun in March 1963 with modification of track plans and the rebuilding of Leeds City Station. The route was to go via Whitehall Junction by construction of the Gelderd curve on a 1 in 50 gradient to connect it with the main Doncaster line. Twenty minutes out of Leeds, the train slows down to pick up commuters from Wakefield.

Rhubarb (Veronica Kelly)

Wakefield: Wars, Wanderings and Waterton

Many restless explorers have left Wakefield, but they usually return. Every 225 stops here, even if it is the 7.10am commuter train with no other stop before London, and there are many passengers; the seats bristling with booked places from Wakefield. The driver has automatic signalling of clear access to the station and the passenger also has reliable warning with the rubbery smell of brakes. The brake system of the 125 is safe but smelly, a problem sorted out with the superseding 225s.

Wakefield Westgate Station is a shadow of its former glory. When it was built in 1867 for the West Riding and Grimsby Joint Railway it was a prominent and audible landmark in the city. A seventy foot high clock rose from an elevated forecourt and was set back ninety-seven feet from the street. The frontage of the station was rich Italianate style designed by J B Fraser of Leeds. The builder of the tower told that the lantern of the brick tower was of cast-iron ribs surmounted by a gilded weather vane, the space between the ribs being partly filled with ornamental cast-iron plates from which hung a bell. The booking hall was graced by a coppered ceiling'. This glory lasted some hundred years and is now demolished to a functional modern building; save for the passenger bridge across the three track line and buildings on the prison side of the tracks. My kindly informant pointed out sombrely that the darkened archway in the centre of these buildings was where detainees entered from HM Prison which is just to the rear. He also suggested I go into the Elephant and Castle pub across the main road from the station where I could see a photograph of the Old Westgate Station hanging above the bar. I did, and saw the clock tower and impressive pillared entrance. Changed as it is approached by train, Wakefield is

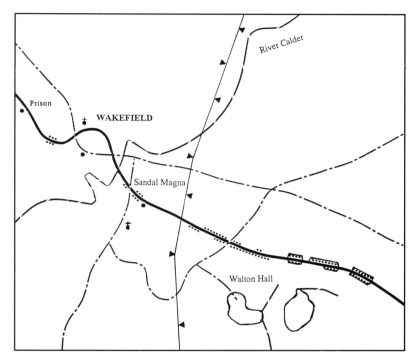

Wakefield to Walton

unmistakable as the platform walls are ornamented with huge bright blue fans of wood, perhaps a memory of the coppered ceiling of the old entrance hall.

Art is also vigorously carried on at the College of Further Education which has regular exhibitions by contemporary artists, and at nearby Castleford the vigour and strength of north-eastern verbal and visual arts is underpinned by the Yorkshire Art Circus. The present is often best understood by historical reference and this is comprehensively taken care of by the Wakefield Museum Services. Here they listen to what you want to know and answer even the most naive questions in a non patronizing way; in a word, they are accessible. There is an almost permanent exhibition of battle as this part of the country has been involved in skirmishes from the Wars of the Roses to Cromwell's time. Soldiers thankfully no longer fight on the soil of Yorkshire but it sends them to the frightening wars of the Gulf, Ulster and former Yugoslavia.

It is popularly thought that "The Grand Old Duke of York, who had ten thousand men" marched them up to the top of the hill on which Sandal castle, two miles south of Wakefield, lies. Although there was a Duke of York in the Battle of Wakefield of 1460, the jingle refers to Frederick, a much later holder of the title and the site of the hill is not known.

The Wars of the Roses refers to the battles over many years between the rival dukedoms of Lancaster, with its red rose emblem, and white rosed York. There was nothing floral or beautiful about these bloody battles. Wily John of Gaunt had seized for his Lancastrian descendants succession to the throne from his rightful older brother's lineage. This worked well enough when the strong Lancastrian Kings Henry IV and V were on the throne, but weak Henry VI, prone to bouts of psychiatric illness, was bound to be the target of Yorkists claiming their right. Weak

18

men marry strong wives and Henry VI was no exception. His queen was an unpopular fierce-willed French woman, Margaret, who was determined to fight tooth and nail to keep power. In 1460, hearing that after the battle of Northampton, Richard of York had proclaimed his son the next heir to the throne instead of her own son, she marched with 18,000 men to Wakefield, with many Yorkist deserters. They joined her, not because they preferred her son, but because he was the rightful heir. The English have always liked legitimacy. Hearing of Margaret's aggression, Richard of York and his son marched to meet her. Margaret took up position at Sandal Common in view of the castle, where she knew Richard was billeted. She also had two other flanks spread out. The superior numbers of the queen and skilful tactics of her generals cut Richard's army to pieces. The fleeing Yorkists were pursued to the death as they ran towards Wakefield. One, Richard of York's eldest son, was caught by Lord Clifford on Wakefield Bridge; he surrendered but was then murdered. Clifford claimed he was justified as his own father had been killed by York at St Albans five years previously. The Duke of York himself was also killed with 2,900 men but although the Yorkists lost their leaders, Edward IV-to-be and his brother, later Richard III, lived. The chapel on Wakefield Bridge that still stands was endowed by Edward IV in memory of his murdered brother and a service is held there each Sunday afternoon.

Two hundred years ago the train could well have picked up Charles Waterton, naturalist and explorer, from Wakefield Station on his way to South America or Spain; but the railway came too late for him and on his journeys westward he left the shores of England at Liverpool.

Charles Waterton was born on June 3rd and died aged 83 on his birthday in 1865. He was the first son of Thomas Waterton, Squire of Walton Hall and from his earliest years displayed behaviour which gave some indication of the brilliance and tenacious perseverance of his maturity. Born into a privileged class he was however a Roman Catholic which had its difficulties in the 18th Century. He was educated at Stonyhurst College by the Jesuits who showed astute sensitivity to his precocious but demanding talents. He was often to be found roaming well out of bounds in his pursuit of natural history and he was appointed chief rat catcher to the school, which post of necessity permitted Charles to pursue rats to their deaths, even if out of school bounds.

He was very attached to his school and spent most Christmases there, grateful to the priests for their inordinate understanding of his need to wander and roam. As an adult he wrote to the school and one of his letters is signed 'from poor Charley the Wanderer', an insight into how a great and successful man felt inside.

Both at the family home with its extensive grounds and at Stonyhurst, Charles Waterton became a knowledgeable naturalist and taxidermist. The grounds of the hall were enclosed by a wall to establish the first nature reserve in the country. His skills with taxidermy have never been improved and his meticulous and laborious methods resulted in preservation of birds and animals that retain their lifelike quality even today. Political opinions are expressed in some of the wickedly humorous stuffed animals that are pushed and pulled out of shape to represent contemporary political figures. Perhaps his most famous taxidermal exploit was to take the skin of the backside of a Howler monkey, treat it with mercuric chloride and many hours of manual manipulation until he was able to indent and pull out the features of a politician he disliked. This 'head' formed the frontispiece to the first edition of his book *Wanderings in South America*, and it is known as a Nondescript.

Walton Hall

His father bought a plantation in South America; those were the days of high colonialism for Great Britain, many of the country gentry owned land in the colonies. Waterton went to British New Guinea (Guyana) and became established as a naturalist and well known taxidermist. Normally a career would have followed with a commission to carry out cartography and exploration work, but Catholicism in those days precluded certain establishment positions which automatically would have been the expectation of a member of the landed gentry. He continued from his own inner momentum the exploration of the hinterland between the Demerara and Essequibo rivers, the search for new animals and made critical observation of his natural surroundings. There are many stories grown almost into legends of the situations in which he found himself, not least when he rode on the back of a South American crocodile, the cayman. Waterton wanted an undisfigured specimen to preserve, and he followed local practice for killing caymans, which was to fire a sort of barbed harpoon down the throat of the animal. The cayman could then be heaved out of the water by the rope attached to the harpoon and killed with arrows. This would have spoilt the skin of it too much for Waterton's purpose so, approaching it cautiously and realising the animal's terror, he leapt on the cayman's back, twisting the front legs behind as a rein. The Indians pulled them in, thrashing tail and all, and Waterton neatly cut the cayman's throat. These events are recorded in contemporary pictures in the Wakefield museum, as is the actual victim of this exploit.

Observant of all that surrounded him, Waterton wanted to investigate the components of South American arrow poisoning which paralysed and killed its victims. It was generally used by Indians on animals and birds in pursuit of food. The substance was known as Wourali and there was ritual and secrecy surrounding its production during which women were excluded.

Eventually Waterton was allowed to witness one of these ceremonies. As well as the active paralysing component from the vine Strychnos Toxifera, there were other non-active additives such as snake venom, ants and magical incantations.

He experimented on the reversibility of Wourali by injecting his donkey with it and afterwards puncturing her trachea and inflating her lungs manually for many hours. She eventually recovered from the paralysing relaxation of all muscles including the respiratory muscles to live to an old age. Waterton realized the medical potential of Wourali in the treatment of rabies which has as one of its symptoms muscle spasm. He offered to treat a Nottingham policeman, but unfortunately the man died before he arrived. Refined and standardised Wourali is the present day Curare, used to produce profound muscle relaxation during surgical procedures.

His scientific reputation was considerable and Charles Darwin came to Walton Hall to meet with him. Sir Joseph Banks, who had journeyed with Captain Cook and was then President of the Royal Society, received Waterton with kindliness and gave him advice on preventive medicine prior to a journey to British Guyana. But Waterton never courted establishment circles and either deliberately damaged his chances by poking fun through taxidermal exploits like the Nonedescript, or never really wanted to be part of them.

Waterton died an active and respected man at his beloved Walton Hall. His funeral procession was over the lake to a spot in the grounds where he was buried between two oaks. The grave is still there, the trees only stumps. Walton Hall built in 1767 and sold by his son Edmund was restored from almost certain total decay by its conversion to a country club and sports centre some eighteen years ago and is now a hotel.

Doncaster: Engineers, Engines and the Eaa

Doncaster is delightful from the friendliness of the waitresses in the Danum Hotel to the careful help given in the reference library.

Just south of the conurbation of Doncaster railway station, it's into the country and through the Yorkshire Wildlife Reserve of Potteric Carr; the two are connected, as the railway, station and Plant Works are built on the drained marshy land of the Willow Carrs. This is how it happened.

In 1639 Edward Pennick of London bequeathed £100 to help the poor of Doncaster and eighteen years later it was decided to use the money to build a duck decoy on Potteric Carr. Profit from the sale of birds caught there would be used for the poor fund, a good way one might think of the rich having sport first, and then giving to the poor. Potteric Carr had been the site of Roman pottery making and was until, its drainage in 1766, a morass of impassable bog and fen with a central mere known as Old Eaa. It was always a place for bird life, bitterns (locally known as Butterbumps) bred there as well as the duck for which it was famous. After drainage it became arable land and with that bitterns departed and the mere was drained in 1790. At that time railways were used for transporting of coal from mining areas and the Middleton Colliery line near Leeds was already running. In the north east George and Robert Stephenson were pioneering lines and engines, the one brother tough and persistent, the other with a sophisticated mechanical grasp. By 1840 the North Midland Railway was running from Derby to Leeds, unconnected to Doncaster save by coach or canal passenger boat. The first temporary station came in 1848 in time for the St Leger and so began the major stake that the town had in the railway industry with her selection as the site of the Great Northern Railway Locomotive works only three years later.

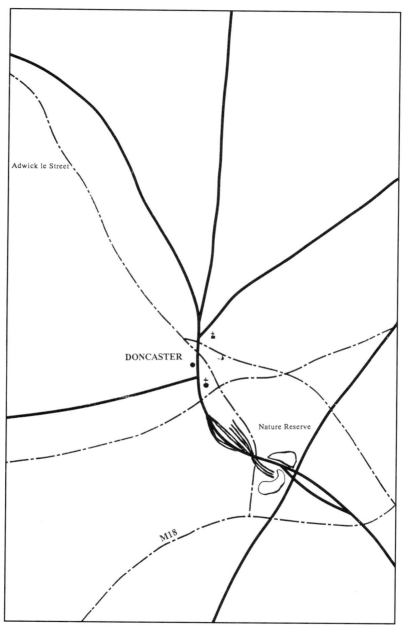

Adwick le Street

DONCASTER

Nature Reserve

M18

Doncaster

25

The great tradition of mechanical engineers associated with railways at Doncaster, Horwich and Crewe began, engineering sheds were built on the marsh lands and sidings laid.

Two men especially were associated with Doncaster, both sons of clergymen, Sirling and Gresley. Stirling's 8 foot express locos (4-2-2) which appeared in 1870 became world famous. Nigel Gresley's ancestors are reputed to have come to Britain as part of William the Conqueror's successful army. A grandson of the solder William Fitz-Nigel de Stafford settled in Drakelowe, Derbyshire but when plague came the family moved to Church Gresley and took its name. Herbert Nigel Gresley, the engineering descendant, was born in 1876 in Derbyshire. By thirteen, this public school boy had drawn a precise diagram of Stirling's 2-2-2 number 234 and so began his life- long association with railways. His first years of working life were at Crewe; needing to study locomotive design he then went to the Horwich works of the Lancashire and Yorkshire Railway. He was there when the first Atlantics emerged, and at 29 he became Chief Mechanical Engineer at Doncaster where he fathered A1, A3 and streamlined Pacifics culminating in the A4 Mallard. Now in 1993 railway sits easily with wildlife. 225s hurtle through the meres, past flocks of teal and gulls with hardly a feather raised. The nature reserve flows over the loop line, although special permission has to be obtained to visit this part of the area.

Down towards the town larger wildlife entertains; the horses of the St Leger. Begun in 1776 country folk flocked to the races and private special trains were run connecting the stately homes of Nostell, Wentworth and Woodhouse to Doncaster. Doncaster has its share of the famous not only on the engineering side; the Poet Laureate Ted Hughes was born at nearby Mexborough; the stage has gained Diana Rigg and Michael Dennison, and sport Freddie Truman and Bruce Woodcock, the boxer.

The Bittern

Retford Station

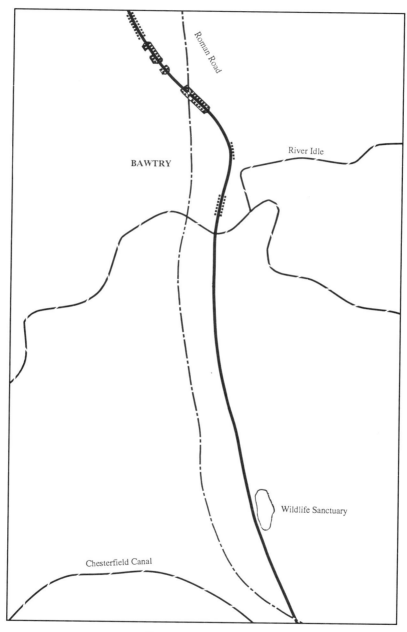

Roman Road

River Idle

BAWTRY

Wildlife Sanctuary

Chesterfield Canal

Doncaster to Retford

29

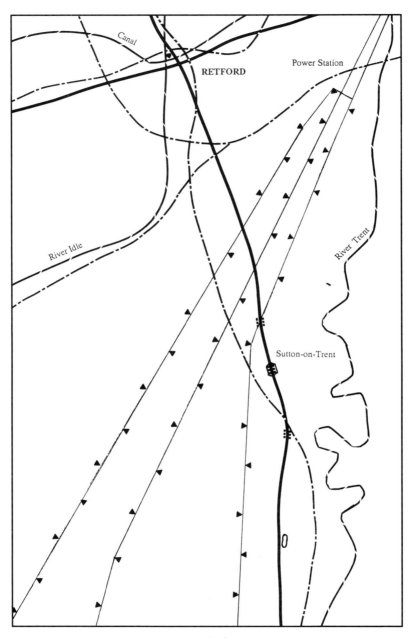

Canal

RETFORD

Power Station

River Idle

River Trent

Sutton-on-Trent

Retford

Retford: Cannons, Canals and Cafes

If Retford is approached from London it's out through Potter's Bar and Watford to the blue flatlands of Peterborough and Grantham and then the land begins to crumple into passable undulations. Retford is really Red Ford, getting its name from the red soil of the settlement established on the banks of the River Idle. It's a town of surprises, with the canal sweeping picturesquely over the river and providing a mooring for pleasure cruisers.

Retford station was built in 1851 by Henry Goodard of Lincoln. It is described coldly as a large Italianate station with Ionic arcaded porticos and complementary end pavilions with an immense length of tediously repetitive gables, but I found the wrought iron canopy of the station roof and the polished brass door plate of the Waiting Room spoke of pride. 'That's the way out,' said the porter as I sized up the platform, wondering where to start poking about first. 'No, I'm just looking round.' He nodded, used to railway enthusiasts. The waiting room still had an Edwardian air, plenty of room and an empty fireplace. Four large pictures decorated the walls; one was a happy scene of a child playing in a park, not an artist's fancy I realised as there was a faded name plate announcing it to be Harrogate; the others were Edinburgh, Jedburgh and Richmond. Next to the waiting room was a ladies convenience of dimensions large enough for a Victorian family. As if abandoned in an outhouse a large pine kitchen table stood ready on which to prop parcels, baby or grandma; a curiosity and a useful one. Here were dinosaurs of railway furniture and long may they survive modern sanitisation.

Station Road leads past the Northern Line Hotel and decaying buildings, relics of past railway animation. Gardens along this road were long, narrow and orderly. Then it was into Queen

Street, right over the canal and river by the footbridge. Following the distant tower of St Swithun's Church as a marker, I entered the bustle of Retford market day. 'Tourist information you want?' Well, you go down Carolgate and into Grove Street. You pass the cannon and it's there, next to the museum,' said the helpful man I asked for directions. 'Cannon?' I thought I'd heard incorrectly. 'Cannon from the Boer War.' And sure enough, as I followed his directions there it was with its plaque, 'Taken at the relief of the Ladysmith. March 1900'.

It is a confusing town as there is East and West Retford. Man has lived here for a long time. Neolithic flint spear heads and remnants of ancient jewellery have been found at Misterton Carr. Newton Cliff nearby has yielded harpoon points and fishermen at Clumber Park found beakers. The Romans had a fortlet named Scaftworth Toma and at Littleborough, where the Doncaster to Lincoln Road crosses the River Trent, a paved ford exists.

In Tudor times the Borough of Retford spent the whole of 12/11d to welcome fourteen year old Mary Tudor, daughter of Henry VIII on her way to Scotland to marry James IV. But the soil of Retford produced more tangible influences on the English monarchy through one of its daughters. William of Orange's queen, Mary, and her sister Anne (the latter to be queen one day) were the great grand-daughters of Anne Denmane, a successful and ambitious offspring of the Lord of the Manor at the Old Hall, West Retford. It was Anne Denmane's grand-daughter Lady Anne Hyde who entered the ranks of the powerful by marrying the Duke of York. So strong was the influence of Anne Denmane that Pepys records in his entry of November 13th, 1661 that the Duke of York was in mourning for the death of his wife's grandmother of West Retford. Retford's strength lay not in getting genes into future monarchs, but at first by agriculture and later by good solid traders such as John Tabron, Rope, Sheep Net and Cover Maker;

Charles the Dyers and Skinner and Johnson's Ironmongers.

The original medieval market place was moved to its present position surrounded by pleasant Georgian houses in the eighteenth century; down Grove Road is a house which was once the residence of landowner and naturalist Pegler. It now houses a museum with a pleasant, easy going atmosphere and is a good source of local information.

There's a shortage of cafes but at one, just off Market Square, cheerful cups of tea are dispensed by waitresses who know the customers they are serving. 'The usual, Jack?' 'Aye, that'll be right.' But outsiders do not get excluded from the friendliness and it is with a smile that the 30p tea is handed over.

I walked back over the river and canal and up Station Road, past the ticket collector and back on to the Northern slow line platform. As I waited for the 225 to Leeds, non-stopping trains thundered through on the fast lanes with hardly a thought for Retford. It is even hard to read the nameplate at 125 m.p.h.

I left Retford, northern bound with a pleasant feeling for this friendly little place with its *Retford Times* and Boer War cannon, and its wall specially built for train spotters. The town has a long railway history: the Retford to Doncaster GNR line was completed on September 3rd, 1849, its distinctive claret coloured carriages pulled by green engines.

Details of cannon, Retford

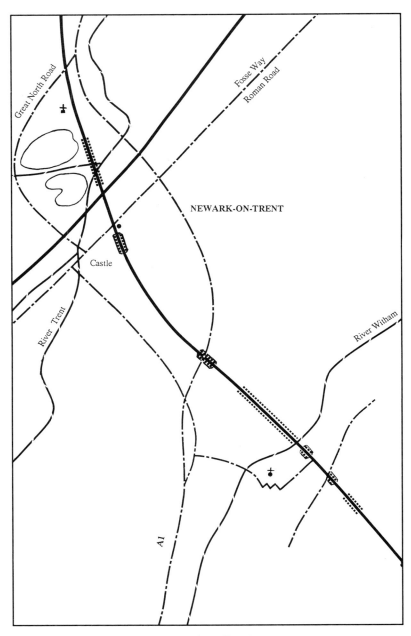

Newark on Trent

Newark: Printers, Peers and Parliamentarians

If the train does not stop and thunders through, it hurtles on the fast track alongside the wrought iron supports to the canopied roof; but if you get out, taxis wait outside or it is a short walk into the town.

Byron knew the town and had his first works privately printed at S & J Ridge, Newark. Known more for the flamboyancy of his short life than the brilliance of his poetry, Byron's contemporary, John Clare, during his insanity, incorporated delusions of being Byron into his persona. Male Byronic stock was rascible. Born in London to a Scottish mother, Byron spent his boyhood in Aberdeen in comparative poverty, but at the age of ten his great uncle died and George Gordon Noel inherited the title. The family seat and lands enabled Byron now to live in genteel poverty at Newstead Abbey near Nottingham, his great uncle having squandered most of the family assets. He is said to have borne his lameness and its painful treatments with youthful bravery at Harrow and Cambridge. This abnormality did not stop his sexual exploits and the little-concealed affairs with his half sister, Augusta, and Lady Caroline Lamb gained him the epithet of mad, bad and dangerous to know. Whether Medora, Augusta's child, was his or her husband, Colonel George Leigh's, will never be known, Byron giving ambiguous and conflicting information on this subject. He married Annabella Millbank but after a year they separated and, continuing his restless ways, he left England to die in Greece aged thirty-seven, fighting for the cause of that country's independence. The printing of *Hours of Idleness* and *Fugitive Pieces* in Newark were the literary beginnings of this rumbustious man. The printing press is in the museum. Poetically insubstantial they may be, more oratory than poetry, but from the beginning they were not ignored, eliciting comments from Shelley, Keats and Goethe.

The Great North Road traverses the town, but modern traffic on the A1 byepasses it. To the north east the Fosseway marches straightly to Lincoln. It was the Prince Bishops of Lincoln who built the castle which dominates the skyline from the River Trent, and here King John died in 1216. During the Civil Wars the town was strongly Royalist and Cromwell punished it by ordering demolition of the castle, but the Norman Gatehouse survives. Pleasure boats ply the river where once wool was shipped to Europe. Newark's merchants dealt with sheep breeders on one hand and Flemish clothiers on the other. Its other staple was coal.

If the castle is the first surprise, the town square is the second; a huge area covered on Fridays by market stalls selling Lincolnshire flowers and vegetables. It is surrounded by historic houses built to have a view of the Church. To a traveller from Yorkshire the Town Hall has a familiar look, it is by the same architect as Harewood House, John Carr. If bear baiting is still carried on, they keep it a secret, but the post is there in the Square. Taverns abound. The oldest, no longer a pub, is the fourteenth century Olde White Hart with its exclusive frontage of twenty four timbered uprights each with a terracotta saint picked out in pink, green and gold; then there is the Clinton Arms Hotel, an important coaching inn on the Great North Road. It was here that youthful Lord Byron stayed while arranging for the printing of his poems at nearby S & J Ridges, printers, an elegant Queen Anne building, now a grocer's. Gladstone's first constituency was Newark and it was from the balcony of the Clinton Arms Hotel that he made his first election speech. He remained the Member of Parliament from 1832 to 1845.

Tourist information are helpful and knowledgeable, and the museum housed in part of the original Magnus Grammar School is a must with its cheerful, unobtrusive keeper who sold me post cards of what I had just seen. Lincoln may be to the east, but westwards it is certainly Sherwood Forest Country and Nottingham. Newark and Nottingham were almost the same size in the Tudor times but the latter now has eleven times the population. As if to demonstrate this modern ascendancy, when I asked two traffic wardens the way, they laughed and said, 'We don't know. We're from Nottingham, love.'

Commemoration plate to Byron

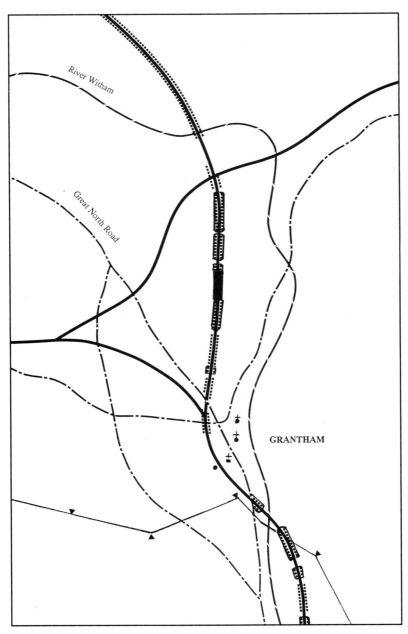

Grantham

Grantham:
Mathematics, Manors and Mermaid Bones

This is the land of big skies from which pylons bear down on the track and accompany it southwards. The man-like marching army of steel comes from the power station at High Marnham.

The Ordnance Survey map gives forward and backward information of these giant's origins and destinations. It is appropriate that these carriers of modern science are so evident round Grantham because this is Isaac Newton country. Born a century before Byron and Waterton, their lives did not overlap and he survived the years to the Great Plague by returning to his birthplace, Woolsthorpe Manor, near Grantham from Cambridge where the disease raged. The manor is close by Roman Ermine Street which is now incorporated in the A1. His father was Lord of the Manor at Woolsthorpe and a moderately wealthy farmer, but died three months before his son's birth. Isaac Newton was educated at the King's School and indelibly carved his signature on a windowsill there. Supposed to be idle at school, perhaps he was not stretched enough academically. Education continued at the Manchester of the Fens, Cambridge, where he evolved the principle of differential Calculus publishing *Principia Mathematica* in 1687. Tradition has it that the apples falling in Woolsthorpe Manor stuck him with the theory of gravity. A modest man, he was reputed to have said he worked out the theories 'on the shoulders of giants'. Three hundred years after the release of his treatise, Grantham held a festival with the catch phrase 'Gravitate to Grantham' emblazoned on an apple. There is an Isaac Newton Shopping Centre and his statue stands on St Peter's Hill. Some say the best view of the town is from the train and as one sweeps from the north over the embankment there is 281 feet of church

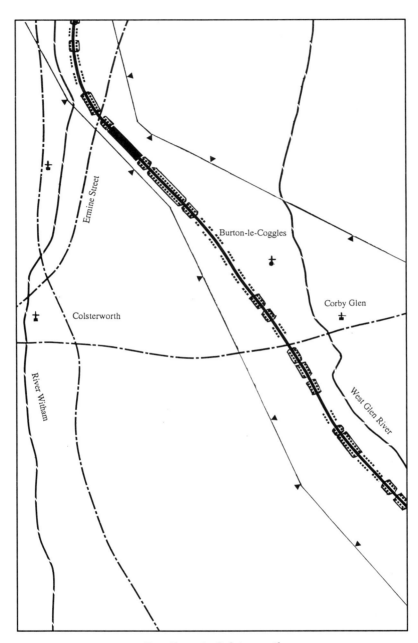

Ermine Street

Burton-le-Coggles

Corby Glen

Colsterworth

River Witham

West Glen River

Grantham to Colsterworth

40

steeple impressively coming into view. Newton knew the Parish Church of St Wulfram and may have questioned to himself the genuineness of the saint's bones preserved as relics in the crypt. History does not relate any comments he may have held when President of the Royal Society on the 'Mermaid's Bone' or 'Unicorn's Horn' which are preserved there.

The mortal remains of the saints were not allowed peace in a grave, but were restlessly carried from one place of worship to another, and the bones of St Wulfram were no exception. The saint born in 650 AD made a mission to Frisia and when William I appointed Ingulgas of Frisia to be Abbot of nearby Crowland in the fens he remembered Wulfram's journey to Frisia and brought the saint's relics to the Abbey. When it caught fire, the relics were brought for safe keeping to the important Saxon Church in Grantham. Its stone replacement had a special upper room built over the north porch for pilgrims to venerate the saint's remains. They are still there.

The Great Northern railway bypassed nearby sleepy Stanford but allowed Grantham to prosper. I visited Grantham on the day of the resignation of Margaret Thatcher and remembered that she was born at a grocer's shop on North Parade on the outskirts of the town.

Back to the station along the featureless road to its back door and once again moving southwards pylons stride on either side. Those on the east side of the line send a posse into Bourne where they bring electricity to the town. It was here that another Prime Minister was born, Disraeli. Unlikely Jewish favourite of Queen Victoria, he was Gladstone's arch rival. Against all prejudices he succeeded to a premiership which had never previously elected a Catholic, a woman or a Jew. A great admirer of Byron, Disraeli shared the foppish predilections of the poet, he also shared his gondolier. When Byron left England for Italy after the collapse of

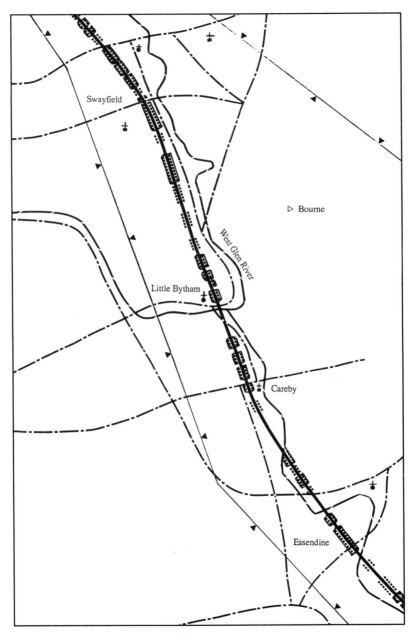

Swayfield

West Glen River

▷ Bourne

Little Bytham

Careby

Essendine

Swayfield to Essendine

his marriage he sold the crumbling Newstead Abbey (now a museum) and with the proceeds rented a great palazzo and also a personal gondolier, Tita. Tita accompanied Byron to Greece and after the poet's death he went to chilly England to work for Disraeli.

Sir Isaac Newton

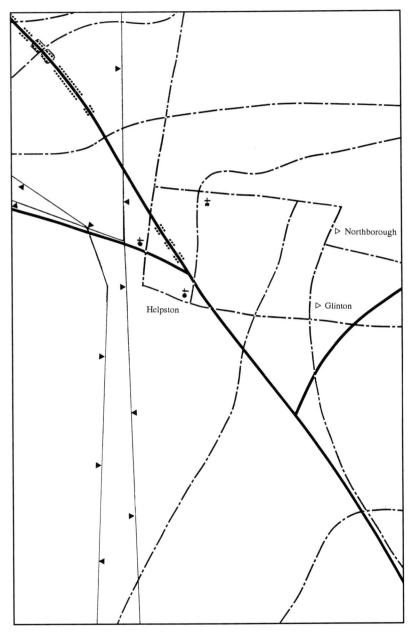

Helpston to Peterborough

44

Monument to John Clare, Helpston

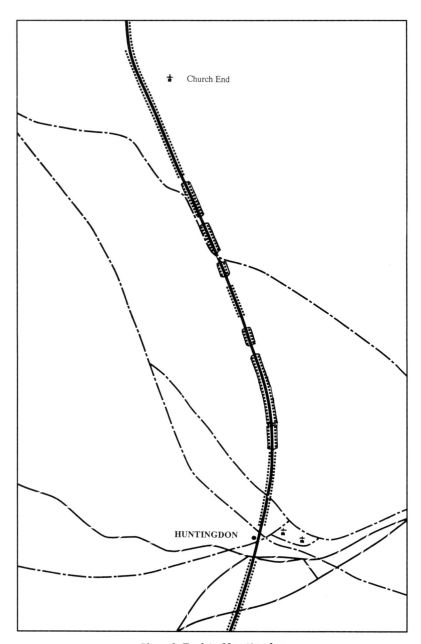

Church End

HUNTINGDON

Church End to Huntingdon

Huntingdon: Daffodils, Decapitations and Diaries

The night mail train stops at Huntingdon and you arrive at Platform 1, where the canopy has lost the decorative wooden fringe of its sister opposite on Platform 2, and the art nouveau lettering over the old restaurant entrance is unilluminated. It is now the station shop and if you arrive in daytime and after school hours, diminutive Maria and her Italian mother serve you. Service is their password; needing two batteries for my camera that came only in packets of four, the two remaining ones were carefully resealed in their plastic bubble by Maria for my future use.

The George is an old coaching inn staffed by courteous females with Elizabethan faces. Imagine the Trust House Forte advertisements, 'Only apply for a job if you are skilled, polite and have a face like one of Henry VIII's wives'. Anne Boleyn was the receptionist who booked me in and showed me to a clean standard room. The medieval gallery outside was floodlit from the old inner courtyard where the ghost of Tom Hernesy, Coachman, moans the passing of coaching days and the coming of the railways that brought him harder times and the new job of driving the two horse omnibus between the inn yard and Cambridge.

Huntingdon is adaptable and a survivor. The old Grammar School educated within the same century Cromwell and Pepys and is now the well-run Cromwell museum. The diarist's life overlapped with nearby Newton in the next county. The museum is all that remains of the 12th Century monastic hospital of St John. There is no charge to go round the reassuringly small museum but donations are gratefully accepted. Strong faces look down from oil portraits of Cromwell's parents and his even stronger faced daughters; there is a friendly air about the museum and what must be priceless pictures are interspersed with memorabilia in an intimate way.

A party of school boys hung round the explanatory text giving information that although Cromwell died of natural causes in his own bed, after the re-establishment of the monarchy his body was exhumed, decapitated and his head displayed on a pole at Westminster for the next twenty years. Real video nasty stuff this, better than tonight's hired cassette. The boys hung round his death mask and listened attentively to the conversation between the Keeper and a visitor.

'The skull is now in Oxford, I've seen it. The nose is crushed as it would be if the body has laid face down in the position for a swing of the executioner's posthumous axe.'

Many throaty noises, gurglings and groans, hands swept horizontally across necks gave evidence that the boys would remember at least one piece of English history. Mrs Jones, the Keeper, was a natural with the boys and told them of one of Pepys' diary entries calculated to appeal.

'January 14th decided to have a wash today, did hands and face but decided to leave neck until another day.'

They were a clean lot from the voluntary aided inter-church School of St Bede's in nearby Cambridge.

'No, I haven't the Ladybird book on Cromwell. Our curator thinks it's a very biased text,' and, turning to me, 'I'm glad you've enjoyed your visit. We've only just re-opened after complete refurbishing. I rather liked the old way of display, but perhaps this is better really.'

I bought a postcard and marvelled at Antonia Fraser's industry in writing yet another bulging biography, this time of course on Cromwell.

If you go on market day in Spring you may get free flowers. As I walked from the museum down the high street the market stall holders were packing up in the rain. A hand cart was piled high with cartons of daffodils and tomatoes, evidently to be thrown away. Yes, they smiled, I could take what I wanted and, feeling slightly like a thief, I rescued an armful of daffodils. The decision as to what to do with them could come later, there was a good bucketful. I left the tomatoes.

Museum, Huntingdon

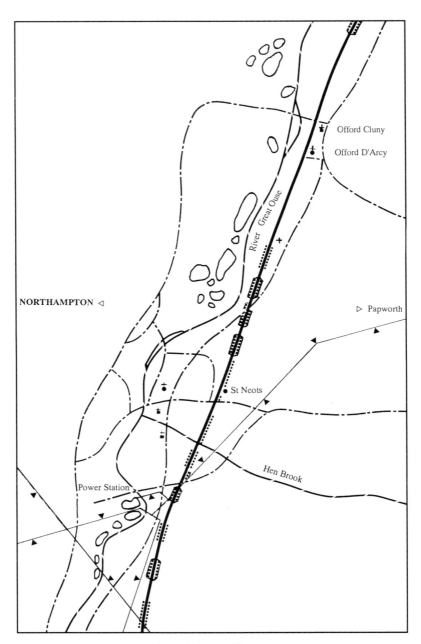

Offord Cluny
Offord D'Arcy

River Great Ouse

NORTHAMPTON ◁

▷ Papworth

St Neots

Hen Brook

Power Station

Offord Cluny to St Neots

St Neots: Postmen, Priories and Paper

Between 1948 and 1952 the White Rose engine pulled the train from Leeds to London in four hours (minus seven minutes). Engineers and managers alike had been preoccupied by reducing journey times in conjunction with preservation of safety. From 1959 an idea germinated of a fast service between north and south on the eastern side of the country but this was halted by the Marples freeze on railway investment. Many problems lay in the way; the engine, carriages and track. The Kestrel engine in 1969 was capable of 125 miles per hour but its brakes were unsatisfactory and eventually it was sold to the USSR, the 125 engine solved this problem but its brakes still smell. The track had to be straightened and widened at certain notorious places. Could engines pull carriages up the infamous High Dyke at St Neots? The curves at Offord would have to be straightened; the work was done in 1970. Modifications made to train and track, the 225 hardly relents in its flight through the town on the Intercity tracks, central to the stopping ones, and the dusty remains of St Neots stir in response.

In 974 AD Earl Leofric and his Countess Leofredda determined to found a priory and current custom dictated that saintly relics should lie under the foundation stone in order to attract pilgrims and encourage worship. Anglo-Saxon chicanery spirited the holy remains of St Neots, a Cornish man, from Neostoke to their new resting place (Cornwall made eternal reproach for the theft to Cambridgeshire by renaming the town St Neots, Cornwall). Meanwhile Leofric's monks established the priory as an entity and obtained a Charter from Henry I for a Thursday market.

I went in search of the Priory, hoping to get information at the

Tourist Information Office. It was a Wednesday and the library which doubled up its function was closed, but the town is well organized. Outside on a wall board was the town's historic trail, and even more fortunately at that moment along came the library's postman. St Neots postmen travel on bicycles and he balanced a large postbag on its handlebars. This unsteadied the bike and it fell.

'Damn!' I moved a little nearer.

'Do you know where the Priory would have been?'

'I would have said something stronger if you'd not been there. Yes, it's round there where the Riverside Snooker Club is.'

Round the corner was an Oast House and the club. The postman wobbled his way round the corner and overturned his bike again.

'Not my day,' he said cheerfully. He posted mail into the Warming Room which turned out to be a coffee house on the site of the Old Priory fire house.

The Great Ouse runs down through Northampton, Bedford, St Neots and out at King's Lynn to the Wash. There's no danger of flooding in the town as an elaborate lock system directs the flow of water into the sea. Cambridgeshire is water land and, as I flicked through a volume on the fens in a bookshop, I learnt that a barrel is twenty-eight gallons. Useful information I thought, better than remembering decalitres and millimetres, even if the old measures had rather odd multiples.

'It's an up and coming place is this town,' said a Scotsman in charge of the camera shop. 'Our industry is paper.' The other one is American airfields in the flat Cambridgeshire countryside.

A year after I had visited St Neots and written the above, the facts that had emerged were validated in another vigorous way; a canoeing trip on the Great Ouse from the paper mills just north of the town at Little Poxton to Huntingdon. The power of the

sluices and locks giving man rule over the river were awesome
seen at first hand as we clambered out to portage the kayaks
round the hazard. The imagination could easily elaborate
circumstances when a small craft could be swept with its
passenger into the flow. Less fearsome and, for the train-o-phile,
very exciting was a ringside view of the 225 thundering past
where the Great Ouse flows along the track; a thrilling inside-
outside perspective on the train.

Oasthouse near the site of Priory, St Neots

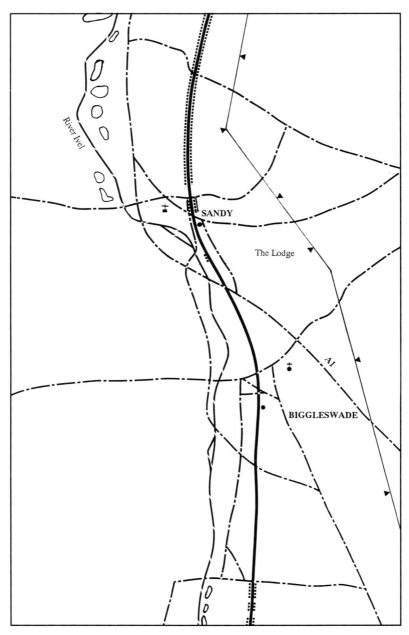

Sandy to Biggleswade

58

Sandy: Owls, Ornithology and Oystercatchers

If you want to go to Sandy there is the local South Eastern network train from Peterborough, past the granaries and into Sandy. The station opened in 1850 but it did not have four tracks then, nor did it have a phone card booth conveniently doorless as it doubles up as the house of the station cat. Fluffy looks comfortable on the dialling box and even purrs when a phone card is pushed in. The vibration of two 125s passing at speed on the central lines did not make him twitch an ear.

Downtown Sandy has a northern feel from pinched faces to friendliness. The market had packets of broken biscuits at three for £1, tomatoes already bagged at 20 pence and a fish stall. I departed with carbohydrate and vegetable but no protein.

Every bird watcher knows that the headquarters of the Royal Society for the Protection of of Birds are at The Lodge, Sandy, Beds, and I went in search of this prestigious centre down Potton Road, back past the station entrance. Now branch bird reserves all over the country hum with activity, run by young professional zoologists for the most part who have chosen field ornithology with its dawn rises and hours of patient observation instead of the warmth of indoor work. Many of them are adorable crackpots, eccentrics beyond the tame of urban life who range their territories with eyes almost as penetrating as their quarries. Some specialize down to a species; one man I met in Devon said he only looked at Oystercatchers, although this must have been somewhat of an exaggeration as there was a comprehensive list of recent bird visitors outside the reserve's building and he was vigorously fund raising by selling iced cake which celebrated the RSPB's anniversary.

But it was odd at The Lodge. Certainly mid-week it was not

crowded and there was an air of poverty abounding. Perhaps all the money goes on the branch reserves for little seemed to be spent here, with the crumbling perimeter wall and the shop full of plastic nick-nacks vaguely connected with wildlife. The post van arrived when I was there but the second post did not yield much. An official from an upper office came down for his letters and looked disappointed where there were none. It was Thatcher's Britain and perhaps preoccupation with the Poll Tax was depriving wildlife of support. A spick and span double decker bus parked outside was in marked contrast to the office, its livery was a twenty foot high owl in spanking new paint.

I decided to take my hat off to The Lodge; it was obviously letting the branches have their leads and develop mini organizations more congruent with local needs. Instead of tweeds and twin-sets, local wardens wore torn jeans and black wellies and any old waterproof coat and there was never a nook or cranny of their reserve that they had not recently paced and placed.

The name Sandy had conjured up a southern Prestbury, a prosperous village of commuters, a place of everlasting sandy holidays, and it was otherwise. From the north, the south is all prosperous and I saw my mistake; maybe this was why Ebenezer Howard had gone for a brand new town in a big way at Welwyn, with covered walks where its inhabitants could say wonderingly, 'It's lovely.'

Oystercatchers (Noel Cusa)

60

The Lodge, RSPB, Sandy

Biggleswade: Pears, Pilots and Puddings

The station entrance is yellow brick and the canopy over the platform stall wears its wooden fridge.   Biggleswade is a diminutive Barnsley; it has a Spastic Society shop and near access to the Shuttleworth Veteran Aeroplane Museum. Each time I hurtle through the station on the central 225 lines I remember Biggles the ace pilot of schoolboy tales, he with the steely grey eyes and the handlebar moustache, the brainchild of W E Johns.

The fictional hero is portrayed as one from a privileged background, eternally young and regarding affairs of the heart of secondary importance to his flying escapades. They were good, clean adventures, whipping up British nationalism against the increasing menace of Germany in the 1930s. Hauptmann Erich von Stalheim, his recurring enemy, was the archetypal menacing German, monocled and suave, typifying an actual threat to the parents of young readers who found those books so compelling.

The flat countryside is spattered with airfields and American personnel are everywhere. In the Dog and Gun at Warden that night there was a table of them eating bar meals washed down with Charles Wells Ale; they were a quietly spoken lot in jeans with accents from Georgia to Washington, not a moustache amongst them. One of them had clear pale eyes but was too short and fat to bear any resemblance to the childhood hero, Biggles. The air crews in the pubs in Bedforshire and Hertfordshire were pleasant, ordinary men, technically sound, trained not to rely on patriotism and good breeding.   In any case, many of their allegiances were instinctively across the Atlantic Ocean.

'Do you know of Biggles?' I asked.

'Oh, those kids books from the 1940s. Sure.'

'Have you read any?'

'Oh, no. American kids read *Electronic Man* and space adventures. I guess British kids do.'

It seemed a millennium away since my annual birthday present was a Biggles book, which was always read the same day or night. Late night hours were always necessary to finish reading the book and it was the one night when my father did not come upstairs and feel the hastily extinguished electric light bulb to see how hot it was.

Midweek in the winter the Shuttleworth Veteran Aeroplane Museum of Old Warden is not busy. It contains eight hangars of early planes and some veteran cars and motorbikes. Richard Shuttleworth, killed in a plane accident in 1940, had been commemorated by his mother with the opening of the museum and although he was not in the RAF, unlike Biggles, he joined up for the Second World War. There are Tiger Moths and Lancasters, Bleriots and Deperdussions standing ready, in flying order, to take off. Alongside them the lethal Dragonfly stood permanently immobilised after the deaths of too many young men. Biggles would quickly have acquired the skills to take off in the first jet manufactured in this country, now a showpiece in the museum; it was probably he who had masterminded the shooting down of the German Air Balloon Zeppelin L31 in 1916 in nearby London, despite the credits to Lt Tempest. German ace Lt Commander Heinrich Mathy lost in that battle could well have been the model for Von Stalheim.

The cafe attendant made her first cup of coffee of the day. 'It's too strong for me. I'd rather have Nescafe myself. If you come on any Sunday in March it is 85 pence for a cup of tea and a slice of fruit cake and it is free entry to the gardens if you go into our museum.' The same care about value for money pervaded this part of the world as in Yorkshire and I felt at home.

Just down the road from the museum is Warden Abbey, the remaining Elizabethan wing of a manor house built on the site of a Cistercian Abbey. It can be rented and restoration inside has restored oak floors and staircase. The finial to the spiral staircase is a wooden pear, the sort of curvaceous object that asks to be stroked; it is a fat desert pear with its stalk intact and is carved all of a piece with the staircase post in solid oak; the undoubted juiciness is at odds with reality. The Cistercians, founders of the Abbey, brought over with them pears; hard, gritty cooking pears that could be pulped to make the ubiquitous sweet compotes used as puddings in medieval times and far too hard to eat raw. The pears became known as Wardens and until very recently people would know that you meant a pear if you talked of Wardens, just as everybody knows a Cox's Orange is an apple. Now extinct, they were the forebears to Parkinson Wardens but their progeny is now outrivalled by modern French competitors. Mrs Bright the local farmer's wife said she liked to think the tree in her garden was a descendant of the original but she actually preferred a good ripe Conference any day. On the morning of departure I lay in bed under the magnificent oak roof, day dreaming of Biggles and pears and ghosts of long dead monks. It was 1990, the winter of the 90 mile per hour gales, and smoke of green willow wood from a torn down tree branch filled the room in a very Elizabethan way.

Then it was back to Biggleswade station with its foot-freezing waiting room on the central platform and walls that stopped short of the ground. There was no inducement to linger. As I waited for my local train to Hitchin, I experienced the holocaust of two 225s passing each other close by on the non-stopping Intercity lines. The nest of air that I had been cushioned in all day was torn away, the muted sounds of people living in a small English town were rent by two rattling, hurtling monsters throwing themselves towards each other as if in menace, only to escape collision by a few feet as they passed at high speed. Each one dashed off into its own distance leaving me gasping but the station master, like a camp guard, was immune and unconcerned; it had happened many times and he'd forgotten the first time he'd witnessed this atrocity of sound. Inwardly I also acknowledged my excitement at the noisy crossing of the trains.

Shuttleworth Veteran Aeroplane Museum, Old Warden

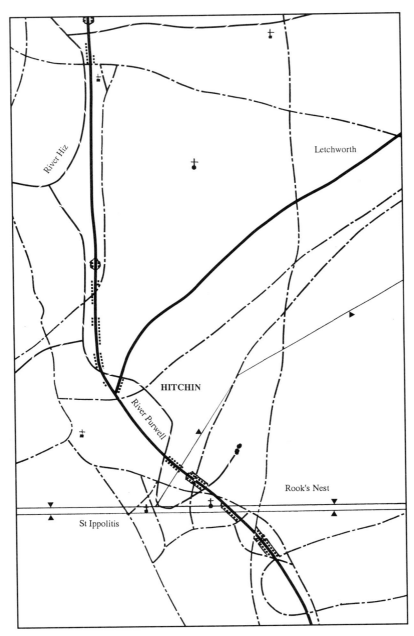

Letchworth

River Hiz

River Purwell

HITCHIN

Rook's Nest

St Ippolitis

Hitchin and Stevenage

Hitchin: Henry, Horses and the Hiz

It is not the white cliffs of Dover, but the chalk cliffs of Hitchin that identify this historic market town as the train rattles through at high speed. If it is the Great Northern stopping train that you have taken and you alight there, there are wooden tassels decorating the canopy over the platforms. The waiting room does not have a fireplace now but it does have a working wall radiator and the ladies has some Edwardian elegance with nice old wall tiles and what must be an almost unique feature - a modern high flush black plastic water reservoir for the loo.

The station is a ten minute walk from the town and used to be across fields when the station was opened in 1850. It had become an important junction by 1857 because here the Midland Railway linked with the Great Northern Line, a union which did not last as they later quarrelled. There is speculation that Hitchin could have become an Horwich or Doncaster if the town had won the contract for railway works, financially an advantage but the town would not have remained a pleasant market town.

History does not relate when the river was named Hiz but it does tell that King Offa of Mercia built a church on the site where St Mary's now is, with the river flowing past the east end and that moderate prosperity grew out of cattle and sheep trading and the sale of fleece and grain.

Henry VIII, who had seized the priory, nearly lost his life twice in the town, the first time when a fire broke out at the Angel Inn where he slept and he fled without even a shirt; the second when hawking, he tried to cross a stream. His stick snapped and he fell with his head in the mud and nearly drowned. His daughter Queen Elizabeth I boasted to a Spaniard that the Hitchin grapes were the best of any country in the world (the present off-licence has a selection of world wines including rare Lebanese wine).

The next century brought decimation in the form of Bubonic Plague to the extent that all the inhabitants of one street died and it was named Dead Street. Cromwell's army passed through and knocked the heads off all twelve apostles which are carved round the font in St Mary's Church.

From the end of the 17th Century an extensive cottage industry grew up as a subsidiary to the fertile grain growth, straw plaiting. There was a Straw Market several days a week and a notice there instructed that 'Plait was to be doubled in half yards and delivered in not less than 10 yard lengths'.

Awareness of exploitation of children's labour was recognised by 1874 when a notice declared that 'plaits from children were not accepted'. The straw plaits were taken to nearby Luton where there was a complementary industry of hat making. The museum has exhibits of unbelievably neat plaits of split straw.

The museum also has very helpful staff that tell you Joseph Lister of antiseptic fame was a schoolboy during his eleventh year at Isaac Brown's Quaker Academy, Hitchin. Born in 1827 in London at the time when bacteria were being recognized as the cause of many deaths, he was much influenced by Louis Pasteur in France and the 'Germ Theory'. He became a surgeon and pioneered the use of carbolic acid, a form of creosote, during operations. Within a year, death from infection fell. Lister's perspective was killing bacteria, not preventing them getting into wounds; sterility during operations was not used and his operation apron was reported to be bloodied and dirty.

The small local hospital was named after him but up the line on the outskirts of Stevenage the modern skyscraper Lister Hospital can be seen from the 225 to the east of the line.

Across the fields at St Ippollits a Roman theologian gave his name to the blessing and good health of horses, the association of the martyr's name perhaps coming from the Greek word 'hippo' for horse. At the Church of St Hippolyts, crusaders from nearby villages came before departure to the east for blessings. Descendants of 12th Century crusaders to the Gulf crisis will not have such curious legends to tell of patron saints of tanks and aeroplanes. The tradition of physic continues with the opening of the William Ransom Physic Garden in 1990 outside the museum. Around the central feature of a pestle and mortar, plants of reputed healing qualities grow in well ordered beds. Here feverfew, the age old cure for weariness, migraine and melancholia, grows; poor John Clare might have found relief in this garden.

Hitchin is firmly linked to the soil. Lavender has been grown for 400 years and was commercially distilled until recently. From the north came two Yorkshire brothers, Robert and John Harkness, who opened nurseries in the town and developed world famous roses such as Ena Harkness, Elizabeth Harkness and Dame of Sark so, while Yorkshire carries away the rhubarb stakes, Hitchin wears the rose crown.

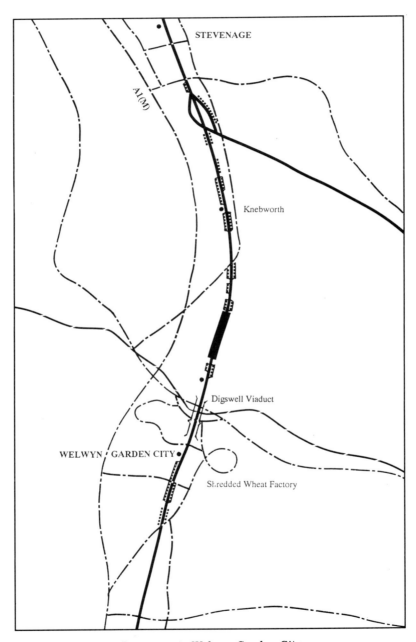

Stevenage to Welwyn Garden City

Stevenage:
Bowls, Brouhahas and Burial Mounds

Do not be fooled by the fact that if New College is the oldest college in Oxford, and New Hall generally is medieval, therefore that Stevenage New Town is old. It is the post-war brainchild of Sir Patrick Abercrombie, planned to relieve overspill from London and if arrival is by train there is a comfortable, wind proof waiting room and a catwalk that leads to the town.

Francis Drake might have been able to watch the Armada while he was playing bowls in Plymouth, passers by on the catwalk can watch senior citizens playing bowls on the indoor green of the Leisure Centre. Bowls was not always the non-contentious affair it is today. In 1541 Henry VIII passed legislation fining keepers of bowling greens and alleys forty shillings for every day's play and expressly forbidding the working class to play at all. This was ostensibly to prevent folk from being distracted from archery practice, but it was actually for fear of the gatherings that bowls attracted with attendant drinking, gambling and conspiracy making. Anything less like a brouhaha could not be imagined down there on the green in Stevenage and I hoped this law of Henry's had been repealed or the Leisure Centre must have accrued large fines. Pleasure loving King Charles II drew up the first set of formal rules for the game in 1670.

Opposite the bowling alley the Gordon Craig Theatre advertised London Contemporary Dance, art exhibitions, coffee and a warm welcome. Then it was down towards the town and there was the Tourist Office in a caravan. The buildings of Stevenage are new but the courtesy of that caravan was traditional and they were even apologetic for charging me 20 pence for a mini guide packed with facts. I was directed to the museum and the Old Town.

From the Great North Road (the A1) looking over to the east are six Roman burial mounds, imaginatively described by local legend as hills created by the devil throwing earth at travellers. After the fall of the Roman Empire, the next wave of settlers built round the church on the site of the old town and named their village Stethenaece (at the strong oak). A market town grew up and then between the 16th and 17th Centuries the high street took on its present appearance. There is no mention of poor deranged John Clare's resting place for the night in Stevenage as he fled on his way home to Northborough. It is well provided with pubs and The Old Elizabethan is a friendly place with a warm fire on a cold February day. John Mabey was installed by it. He had a face of a thousand furrows and a knowledgeable air.

'Not what it was in the thirties. You could walk over fields to St Andrew's and St George's Church, where the museum is.'

He had been the kitchen boy at Rook's Nest, the childhood house of E M Forster.

'After he left, it was bought by the Postons; lots of music composed there, you know,' he said. In fact a great deal of composing altogether had taken place there as Forster had put memories of the house straight into his book *Howard's End*.

'Lots of literature in these parts, those Londoners think we're all elementary school types here, or computer wizards. Never give us credit for enjoying a good book in Stevenage. George Bernard Shaw lived just south of there at Ayot St Lawrence.'

Typically, George Bernard Shaw had flamboyantly named his house *Shaw's Corner* and lived there for over forty years. Obscurity was not his hallmark and, as he wrote *St Joan* and *Mrs Warren's Profession*, the famous came to argue with him. Ellen Terry and Mrs Patrick Campbell were no strangers to *Shaw's Corner* and Garrard, one of Captain Scott's party to the South

Pole, asked Shaw for a title to his book about the expedition; the suggestion was *The Worst Journey in the World*.

'I wasn't really a monarchist,' said John Mabey, 'until Maggie contended for the throne, but I've always had a soft spot for the Queen Mother. You might think, you coming from that part of the world, that she was born up north, she being a Bowes-Lyon, but you'd be wrong. She was born just across the A1 at the St Paul's Walden. Who do you think will be the leader of the Conservative Party now she's gone?'

'Hard to say,' I said non-committedly, not wanting to get into politics.

'Anyway, I'm off now. Got to catch the bus down to the bowling green. I'm in a competition this afternoon.'

He went out and hidden from view where he had been sitting was a rectangular plaque on the wall stating 'Tom Goode was here'. Expecting another literary tale, I asked the barmaid. She smiled. 'It's just someone who sat there a lot and his friends clubbed together to put it there.'

Stevenage old town was still forging new traditions, but the plaque did not look very durable. Modern recorder of births, marriages and deaths, the Registry Office, is down the road. Once it had been the Old Swan Inn, well known to Samuel Pepys who made several visits in the 1660s.

Hatfield: Larches, Lies and Lords

Associations with scheming, imprisonment and bullying are the history of this town, as well as horticulture, grandeur and power. Even as the 125 speeds to the east of the line, the central cupola and chimneys of Hatfield House can be seen.

In 970 King Edgar of Mercia gave Hatfield to the Benedictine monks of Ely, the monastery was converted to a bishopric and Hatfield was known by the administrative name of Bishop's Hatfield. At the end of the 15th Century a palace was built by Bishop Morton for his residence. There are substantial remains of this building close to the Parish Church of St Etheldreda, the patron Saint of Ely. The palace became Crown property after the dissolution and in it Mary Tudor and her half-sister Queen Elizabeth I spent years of their childhood under conditions close to imprisonment. During the reign of James I the family most closely associated with Hatfield, the Cecils, were invited to take it up as a residence. Robert Cecil found the Old Palace gloomy and old fashioned so used the material to build himself a new palatial house in 1607, the towers of which can be seen from the train.

It might be wondered what that serviceable house plant Tradescantia has to do with Hatfield, but grand houses need assiduous gardeners and Robert Cecil, Lord Salisbury, Lord Treasurer of England employed John Tradescant the Elder as his gardener. This man was no ordinary jobbing digger but a traveller, collector of curiosities and introducer of many plants into England, and on him and his son and daughter-in-law was perpetrated one of the all time tricks of history; of this later. The unusual name of Tradescant is not exotically foreign, the elder John is thought to have ornamented the name of Tradeskin to its more decorative form. He was sent on plant hunting journeys by his employer and brought back mulberries from France with the aim of introducing silk-weaving into England. He is reputed to have introduced the Cos lettuce and brought vast numbers of vines from France for the establishment of a vinery at Hatfield. If Hitchin bears the accolade for roses in our times, Tradescant searched France to collect them in his time. He then moved from Lord Salisbury's employ to live in Kent, but contact with the powerful of the land was established and he again set out on plant hunting expedition. He went to Archangel in Russia and from there brought back the first larch seeds to be introduced to this country. He compared the soil of Russia to that of Norfolk, the ploughs to those of Essex, and the carts to those of Staffordshire. The journey was undertaken over the summer of 1618 and these comparisons might not have been so easy over the icy months of winter.

Eventually on the death of his employer, the Duke of Buckingham, he entered the service of Charles I and his Queen, Henrietta Maria, and began the establishment of his physic garden and museum at South Lambeth, London. Always a collector of oddities, he had amassed a vast collection and bought a house which became known as Tradescant's Ark. It is recorded that he was making enquiries about unicorn's horns, which proved to be merely the snout of a fish, but,even so, very precious against poisons. He died before being able to take up his post as first keeper of the newly opened Oxford Botanic Garden.

A son of a great man often loses the acquisitions of a great father but, although this happened, John the Younger was no lightweight. The tree most associated with the streets of London owes its presence to him as on one of his three voyages to Virginia he introduced the Occidental tree which, crossed with the oriental Plane, produced the London Plane; he also introduced the Acacia and Lilac. On return from his last visit abroad he published

Tradescantia (Veronica Kelly)

Museum Tradescantianum, the first catalogue from a public museum to be printed in England. He dedicated it to the president and fellows of the Royal College of Physicians. It also included a list of all the plants introduced into the Lambeth Garden by the Tradescants.

The museum was a jumble of objects, one of which was the Dodo whose head and foot is now in the University Museum of Oxford. Among the helpers and donors to the museum of Lambeth was Elias Ashmole and it looks as if quite early on in their acquaintance this man was casting avaricious eyes on the collection, as the Tradescant male line finished with the death of John the Younger's son. John II had intended the collection to pass to the Crown but a 'Deed of Gift of all his Rarities' was drawn up in 1657 leaving Ashmole the entire collection. His Will of 1661 makes his second wife Hester sole executor and bequeathed his 'Closet of Rarities' to her, but to pass to the University of Oxford or Cambridge after her death. He died in 1662 and two years later the vultures were settling. Ashmole contested the Will and a Court case settled in his favour after the death of Mrs Tradescant. The harassment of this widow in her fifties by the ambitious Ashmole can be imagined and he records that she was willing to deliver up the rarities to him, several of which he carried to his house, a few days later removing the remainder. He announced his intention to present them to the University of Oxford so long as a suitable building could be erected to receive the exhibits. In 1678 the widow was found drowned in her pond and the same month Ashmole removed the rest of the pictures from her house. Sir Christopher Wren was the architect for the Ashmolean museum, the collection was transferred there in 1683 and the name of 'Tradescant was unjustly sunk in that of Ashmole'.

However Tradescant, sometimes of Hatfield, is commemorated in the group of plants known as spider worts;

wandering jaw, or wandering sailor and more commonly just Tradescantias. John the Younger's visits to Virginia are remembered specifically in Tradescantia Virginiana.

In the nearby church three prime ministers are buried; Robert Cecil (who Pepys noted he had seen on attending the church), Lord Melbourne (who's wife swooned over Byron) and Robert Gascoyne. In the old town of Hatfield, tradition has it that Bill Sikes (who murdered his wife Nancy in Dickens' *Oliver Twist*) went for a quick one at the Eight Bells Inn.

Shredded Wheat Factory

Welwyn Garden City:
Viaducts, Victorias and Valleys

It is easy to locate Welwyn Garden City from the 225 because the Nabisco factory producing *Shredded Wheat* clearly announces its presence. The characteristic shape of the Louis de Soissons 1925 building was until recently on every packet of the breakfast cereal. The lady ticket collector replied to my questions concerning the whereabouts of the library and the town by saying in an Irish brogue, 'It's lovely.' Ebenezer Howard, its founder, must have turned contentedly in his grave at this statement for it was he and men like him, appalled at the living conditions of the working classes in the 1920s in the crowded slums of London, who wished to develop garden cities and suburbs. Welwyn Garden City extends on both sides of the railway. To the east and close to the railway lies the industrial area, for a garden city unlike a suburb must possess enough industry to ensure an independent life. To the west of the station is the civic area with shops and public buildings and the covered Howard Precinct in tribute to Ebenezer Howard. Started in the southwest quarter, it now extends over the whole area.

Directly to the west of Welwyn Garden City on the north bank of the River Lee there are connections with Byron, at Brocket Hall. Here two Prime Ministers died, Lord Melbourne and Lord Palmerston, and it was the setting for the scandal between Melbourne's wife Lady Caroline Lamb and Byron. The poet was the talk of his day and his fame as a womanizer seemed to draw women to him. Caroline Lamb wrote a novel in which Byron was the hero, and eventually she met him at a party and became infatuated with him. He flirted openly with others and had a long-standing affair with his half-sister, Augusta Leigh. It is

79

reported that some fifteen years later she saw a funeral procession passing northwards and, on asking who was dead, was told it was Byron. She became mentally ill and died four years later. After her death, her husband, released from her histrionic behaviour, became Prime Minister twice, becoming guide and mentor to the young Queen Victoria. Brocket House still belongs to the Brocket family and is also a residential conference centre.

The whole development was made possible originally by acquisition of land from the private estates of Lord Salisbury of Hatfield and Lord Desborough of Panshanger. Although Hatfield House remains intact, Panshanger was pulled down because of the development and because the Lord had no male heirs and his two daughters did not want it. The name remains associated with the airfield and part of the industrial estate. The Mimram River forms the northern boundary to Panshanger and, because of this valley, one of the many astounding feats of railway architecture was built, the Digswell Viaduct, immediately south of Welwyn North Station. It was built in 1850 and on August 25th, 1851 Queen Victoria travelled on the railway to Balmoral. Reaching Digswell Viaduct she became nervous and insisted on stopping the train and crossing the valley by coach, regaining the Royal train at Welwyn North Station.

Blondin, who crossed the Niagara by tightrope blindfolded and pushing a wheelbarrow was less intimidated and used the Mimram valley as a training area.

The viaduct has forty, 30 foot-span arches, 98 feet from the river at the highest point and is 500 yards in length. It took two years to complete and has several times been strengthened and added to. The outer skin of blue facing bricks were put there in 1935, the bars were provided to reinforce the two brick skins in 1965 and drains and waterproofing were added in 1986. So the viaduct has developed alongside the high speed trains.

The bank of the Mimram to the west of railway track led to an exciting find in 1960. An archeologist found Roman tiles there, the remains of a complex of four buildings on a site at Dickets Mead. Today there is one feature that can be viewed, the third century bathhouse which has been preserved in a specially constructed vault directly under the A1(M). Exit from this road driving northwards is at Junction 6 where a sign reads 'Welwyn A1000', then follow the side road straight over the first roundabout. Watch out for a sign saying 'Welwyn Roman Bath House' on the right of the second roundabout.

Over to the south west of Welwyn is St Albans, well fought over site of many a battle. Here Boadicea grappled with the Romans in the fighting that eventually lead to her defeat and death. Her name means Victory, but victory was not to be her's. Queen of the Iceni, a tribe of Britons centred in East Anglia, she was the widow of a king who died in AD 43 and who made little mark on history. The stories of her exploits are exaggerated but exist she did. Reliable descriptions have portrayed her as tall with long, flowing red hair. To the Romans, who were dark haired southern Europeans, all brown haired Britons were described as red heads, perhaps to distinguish them from the northern Europeans who were blond. Boadicea's chariot, the wheels of which legend tells had knives attached to mow down opponents, is unlikely to have been fact as they would have been an equal hazard to her own army. Fired with hate against the invading Romans because of the rape of her two daughters by them, the three of them caused havoc in the well-disciplined Roman army at St Albans before their final defeat. This city was also a battle site in the later Wars of the Roses.

My next stop southwards was Potter's Bar and I left Howard's vision of a city. He lived and died there in 1928 to be buried further north in Letchworth Garden City cemetery.

81

Cromwell

Potters Bar: Gates, Graves and Germans

The coming of the railways destroyed the turnpike roads but it could also be said that the healthy competition of a competing system did a lot to force improvement on them.

People talk about the Great North Road but this was somewhat of a misnomer; the ancient road from London to the north was through Waltham Cross, Ware and Royston, much of it along Ermine Street, an ancient track upgraded by the Romans. The road through Potters Bar and Hitchin was an alternative, used by Pepys and another diarist from Leeds, Ralph Thoresby, who made business trips between Leeds and London in the 1690s. There were these two roads, the north road through Ware and the south road through Potters Bar. Unlike the railways, the north road developed on existing tracks and sometimes had to make do with east and west connecting roads resulting in double bends on it at Hatfield and formerly at Potters Bar. The name 'North' implied a road going north, not a planned route north from London to York, and could equally refer to the destination of St Albans or York or Carlisle. It was at first the great North Road which Daniel Defoe referred to in connection with Huntingdon, not the Great North Road; that came later.

The same connotations of the Great Northern Railway still exist, which is the line that runs to Royston and Cambridge. However, back to the Potters Bar and the turnpike system. Wheeled traffic between towns started about 1650 and did much damage to the roads of that period, which were at best simply wide paths with some gravel spread on them. Responsibility for repairing them lay with the men of the parish. Some of the small parishes lay along routes used by heavy waggons and a system was introduced between 1663 and 1702 to charge for this type of

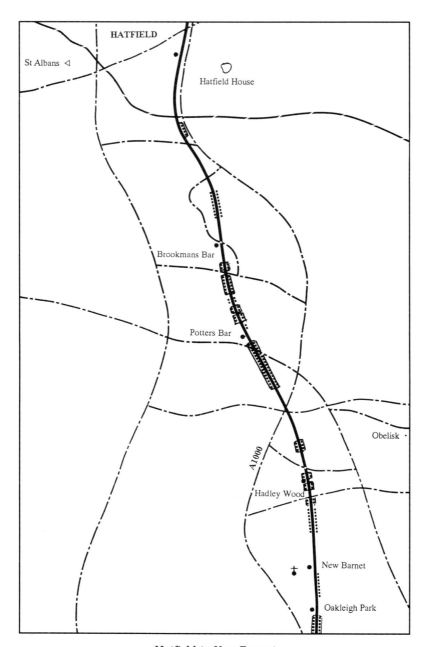

Hatfield to New Barnet

traffic, while making little or no charge to local traffic, pedestrians and horse riders; the money raised was used to maintain the roads. Charges were levied at carefully sited gates which were known as turnpike gates, but there were other gates which marked the boundary of estates through which the road passed. At first Potters Bar had such a gate, but it became a turnpike road with more gates in 1730. Travellers could easily avoid and bypass the gates to avoid the tolls, which usually existed at sites about ten miles apart. The toll gate in Potters Bar has been moved several times to accommodate new road developments, but the building at the junction of the High Street and the new Hatfield Road still exists.

Customers on the 125/225 can well visualize as they journey in two hours from Leeds to London the excruciating rigours of a coach journey some six miles between Hatfield and Potters Bar which, if the passenger was lucky, might last the same number of hours. Where trees overhung the road they might provide shade in the summer but more to the point prevented the road drying after wet weather. Eventually mobilised by railway competition, moves were afoot to build new roads and the engineers associated with these projects were Telford and Sir James McAdams (son of the inventor of the tarmacadam road surface). They planned a new north to south road which would follow a line from Barnet to Hatfield roughly where the Barnet bypass was built many years later, leaving Potters Bar in peace. The High Street is fifteen minutes' walk from the station.

Commotion came in another form later, from the skies. Imperial Germany's Zeppelin campaign on Great Britain during the First World War began in 1915 and reached its climax the following year. The south part of the country suffered greatly. Britain's air defences, previously non-existent, had improved sufficiently to make the struggle if not equal then at least contestable. On September 2nd, 1916 the first German airship was shot down on British soil.

The Kaiser had planned to raise London to the ground by means of his 'Iron Thunderstorms', a term used by the German press to describe the Zeppelins (the airships). These were manned craft of destruction, unlike the Second World War scourge, the Doodle Bugs. However, an event in Potters Bar on October 2nd, 1916 was the culmination of British retaliation to stop this form of attack. The Commander of the German crew on board the Giant Zeppelin of that night was Kapitan Heinrich Mathy and he led a fleet of eleven. The weather was bad, squally over the North Sea and the craft were floundering, encrusted with ice, but Mathy was tracked resolutely proceeding south-southwest to North London. He was caught in the scanning beam of a solitary searchlight and he tried to avoid it by veering to the north-west. British defence was to send an intercepting plane to shoot down the German Zeppelin. Second Lt Wulstan Tempest with his black-domed BE 2c biplane was commanded to stand by and subsequently take off to pursue the German craft which, held in the pyramid of British searchlights, was in trouble. Mathy off-loaded all his bombs to lighten his craft, causing considerable damage in Cheshunt, and attempted by twisting and wheeling to break free of the searchlights. Tempest fired his Lewis guns at the German, the L31 Airship glowed red, flames shot out as she fell to the ground at Oakmere Farm, Potters Bar, miraculously missing the density of the small town. Ammunition exploded with the wreckage and it was some time before approach could be made despite the endeavours of the New Barnet fire engine. The bodies of the German naval officers were recovered. One of them bore the ribbon of the Iron Cross and, when his thick, woollen muffler was pulled aside, he was recognised as the great German commander, Mathy.

It was a bitter war and British pleasure at what happened in Potters Bar that night was understandable. Crowds flocked from London to the site by road, rail and even roller skates; the hate engendered by two bitter World Wars involving the Germans is slow to die. The bodies of the Germans had to be buried and it was done in great secrecy in unconsecrated ground at Potters Bar cemetery; the coffins were taken down Mutton Lane on a Royal Army service lorry with the commander on a separate trailer. They were buried alongside their compatriots killed a month earlier in the S1-11 Airship. A hundred men of the King's Royal Rifle Corps paraded, the Last Post was sounded and an aeroplane flew low overhead; the burial was conducted by an Army chaplain and the Vicar of St Mary's, Potters Bar. The bodies were not to remain there.

In July 1926 the widow of Mathy, Hertha, visited his grave. She was dismayed to find it neglected and segregated from British graves by wooden lattice work. She laid a wreath and was received sensitively by the undertaker. But next day he warned her that the people of Potters Bar objected to the wreath. After her unhappy visit she complained to the German Ambassador about the neglect of all the German graves and so, very speedily, headstones were erected to replace decaying wooden crosses and shrubs planted. There was no further maintenance and in 1930 members of Potters Bar TOC H were so appalled at the condition of the graves that they restored the plot without official approval. International relationships were improved each Armistice Day due to co-operation between the German Ambassador and the Jobmaster of TOC H, but still Nazi influence was gaining ground in Germany and the religious service became the arena for some young Germans giving the Nazi salute. By 1935 it had become an excuse for Fascist demonstration from British as well as Germans and the last ceremony took place in 1939. The new German

Ambassador von Ribbentrop turned up late and tried to park outside the cemetery gates against parking regulations. The widow of the retired head postman who lived there stormed out and told him to clear off. The mighty Ribbentrop got back in his Mercedes and was driven away.

In September 1962 the bodies of the airship crewmen were exhumed and re-interred in the newly dedicated German War Cemetery at Cannock Chase. Mr Leslie Birt, son of the undertaker who officiated at their original funeral in Potters Bar, said quietly, 'Poor old Mathy, gone for good now. Well, it was all due to the war, wasn't it? And we've had enough of war, haven't we?' An ironic comment on January 9th, 1991 on the eve of further bloodshed in the Gulf, as I write this chapter.

Then it is back from these gloomy thoughts, down the High Street and right at The Walk to the modern 1955 station designedby N Powell and on to the train to pass the sand coloured office blocks with their large grey framed windows and the high pitched roofed houses and it is almost straight into the tunnels before and after Hadley Wood Station and on to Barnet.

Iron bridge over canal, Retford

Chantry Chapel, Wakefield Bridge, scene of murder of Duke of York's son, 1460

Hadley Wood and Barnet:
Feuds, Friendships and Fighting

The real north/south divide of England could be defined as: every Southerner knows that Barnet was the site of one of the decisive battles of the Wars of the Roses where Warwick the Kingmaker was slain; while every Northerner knows that Pontefract Castle was where Richard II was foully murdered, and that Wakefield Bridge in 1460 saw the mean slaughter of the Duke of York's eldest son, the boy having already surrendered. Both battles of Barnet and Wakefield were part of the rumbling rivalries between the dukedoms of York and Lancaster. The difficulty in understanding the competition and divisions between two houses is partly because both the Dukes of York and Lancaster were descendants of the same man, Edward III, and the cousins feuded over their rights to the throne of England.

The social medieval scene for the Battle of Barnet in 1470 was complex and involved family feuds, ambitions for the crown and endeavours for the vast fortunes that accrued to lords rewarded with land and money for loyalty to the king. Shakespeare simplified the situation by arguing poetically that the Wars of the Roses were only a struggle for the Crown. The plays of Henry IV and Henry V accurately characterise these kings as strong men who gathered about them powerful lords, ensuring support by endowments of dukedoms and land, support that ensured maintenance of the crown on their head. The family trees of medieval monarchs are a snakes and ladders board of up and downs, guile and intrigue, and not the more-or-less ordered succession of the 20th Century.

The House of Lancaster was represented by Henry VI who was weak, mentally unstable (probably suffering from periods of depressive illness) and married to the disliked Margaret of Anjou. The couple had no child and the King's cousin, the Duke of York, was heir to the throne until, after eight years of childless marriage, on October 14th, 1453, Margaret gave birth to a son, Edward. The Queen planned and plotted to become Regent for her ailing husband and their underage son. This polarised the Lords even more as Margaret was generally disliked and the Duke of York gained greater following, and eventually it was he, not Queen Margaret, who became Protector for the throne. By the following year the King was mentally stable and York's commission as Protector lapsed. Power struggles continued, culminating in a bloody battle at St Albans between Yorkists and the Lancastrian King, where great bloodshed was added to the family feuds. Warwick (the Kingmaker) had allied himself to the Yorkists on the battlefield where in those times kings, queens and dukes were actually at the head of charging cavalry leading their soldiers into battle, and after the defeat of the Yorkists Queen Margaret ordered confiscation of land from the defeated lords, this fermented continuing hostilities. Warwick and the Earl of March (the future Edward IV) rose up and took the King prisoner. The Duke of York then put forward the claim of his family to the throne, based on the illegal seizure in the past by a younger brother, John of Gaunt, for his son Henry IV. The complex matter of succession was solved by agreement that Henry VI would remain King for his lifetime but his son would not succeed him and the throne would then go to the Duke of York (in the event Henry VI's son died in his youth).

Queen Margaret continued the dispute and won the Battle of Wakefield in 1460, killing the Duke of York. The situation was reversed in Towton, Yorkshire when the deceased Duke of York's son, Edward, Earl of March and Warwick, defeated the Royals; Queen Margaret, the King and their son fleeing. Edward was proclaimed King, although uncrowned, while Henry VI was a prisoner in the Tower; England had two kings. The Duke of Warwick continued his support of Edward IV until he was snubbed by the King choosing the widow of a Lancastrian Knight as his queen rather than a French princess negotiated by Warwick the Kingmaker. A further battle with an army now led by Warwick against Edward defeated the King who fled to France. Henry VI was brought out of the Tower and replaced on the throne. Six months later Edward returned from France and Warwick, leading the Lancastrians from the north, barred Edward's advance from the south at Barnet.

As the train dashes through Hadley Wood and Barnet southwards one can picture precisely the battle that ensued. Warwick had 15,000 men in three groups on fields through which the A1000 now runs. The right flank of the army was behind a hedge which still exists along the right-hand side of the fairway of the third hole of the Old Ford Manor golf course. The stems of some of the boundary hedges are eight inches across and may be contemporary with the battle. The middle section of Warwick's army was astride the main road and he himself commanded the left wing out to the east of Hadley Green. Edward marched out of London with 10,000 men, he was one of England's most able kings and perhaps the best royal general there has been, according to Howard Green. Edward's army was disposed in three sections, himself in the centre and the right flank very near the present Hadley Wood Station facing Warwick. On Easter Sunday in thick fog the northern Lancastrians advanced southwards and routed some of the Yorkists back into Barnet town. With the lack of visibility Lancastrians fought Lancastrians. Edward made a cavalry charge between the Lancastrian flanks to seize their rear. Warwick's army slowly gave way and eventually dissolved completely. Warwick, still on foot having foolishly left his horse far back, tried in medieval armour to run into a wood for safety. He was inevitably caught, thrown to the ground, his visor prised open, recognised and instantly killed. This most respected, loved and able man, one of the greatest leaders in English history, had been defeated by the greatest general of his age, Edward IV, then only 21 years old.

Warwick the Kingmaker's death on April 14th, 1471 is commemorated by an Obelisk erected in 1740 at Hadley Highstone on the northern fringes of Barnet.

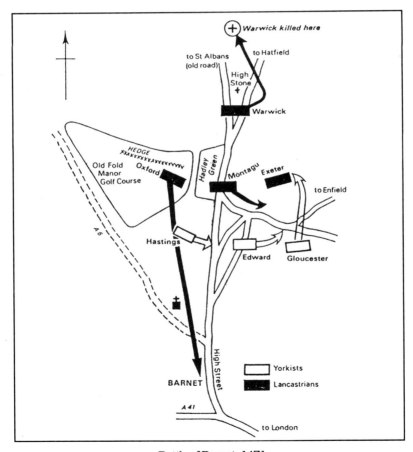

Battle of Barnet, 1471

London King's Cross:
Facades, Fish and Funerals

The capital is within commuting distance of Leeds and many of the briefcases carry their owners three or four times a week to the taxis and underground. Alexandra Palace, Barnet, Wood Green and the red and green bridge of Finsbury Park have whistled past, but the 225 stops at none of these; country aunts and cousins visiting their relatives in north London must travel back north by local transport. It is into the tunnel and here is King's Cross, once a country crossroads in King Henry VIII's time.

Round to the right as I throng out with the crowds I think of Boadicea, sickened, shamed and defeated by the Romans, taking poison with her daughters on a field now below the concrete of Platform 10.

Behind the station is Regent's canal, once a busy commercial waterway with links to all parts of the country, it was superseded by the railways. Out of the station and turn left into York Street and follow the perimeter wall up to Maiden's Lane Bridge and descend by the steps down to the canal. It was developed as a link between the Grand Junction Canal at Paddington and London Docks in the east. As with any other development there was controversy but Thomas Hood, whose brainchild it was, wisely enlisted the support of famous John Nash. Nash was well placed as a friend of the Prince Regent to obtain permission for its execution and he had just turned part of the late King Henry VIII's hunting grounds into Regent's Park. The canal could circle the park. In 1812 the Regent's Canal Act was passed, a company was formed to build it and an architect appointed. On August 1st, 1820 a well decked crowd flocked for its opening and there was competition for prime canal side wharfs. By 1840 Thomas

Pickford, now part of the huge Pickford removal business, had the largest fleet of boats on the canal numbering 120.

Everything has its heyday and in 1837 the first main line railway in London opened at Euston bringing a slow and steady diminution in canal traffic. A century later after the Second World War, just as the end of ammunition transport meant closure of a branch railway line in Yorkshire at Thorp Arch, peace brought commercial traffic to an end on the canal.

It remains a huge rural resource for overcrowded London. People walk and jog along the towpath, they sail their boats and live in them. And there is the great national sport of fishing. At weekends competitions take place and silently under umbrellas and with all the paraphernalia of worms, nets and bran, reputations are made. There's pike, perch and roach to be coaxed by clever fishing guile.

And if you will there's the whole panoply of London to visit: the Royal Society of which Isaac Newton was the president, and the Royal Mint of which he was master. Down in the City the haunts of Pepys can be followed from his diaries and by Lambeth Palace justice has finally been done to the Tradescants by the opening of the Museum of Gardening on the site of their residence. Back up in North London in Highgate there are memories of the funeral procession of Byron, the body back on its way up north for burial in Nottinghamshire. Still youthful, Mary Shelley and Ann Williams, widows both of the sailing tragedy that had drowned their husbands, stood as living relics of the expatriate set which had left England and lived together in Italy; Shelley and Byron had been friends.

Byron

So we'll go no more a-roving
So late into the night.
Though the heart be still a loving
And the moon be still as bright.

For the sword out wears its sheath
And the soul wears out the breast,
And the heart must pause to breathe,
And love itself have rest.

Though the night was made for loving
And the day returns too soon
Yet we'll go no more a roving
By the light of the moon.

Sources of information:

England in the Later Middle Ages, M H Keen

Ark to Ashmolean, 1983, Arthur MacGregor, Ashmolean Museum, Oxford

Hertfordshire Curiosities, 1980, John Lucas, Dovecote Press Ltd

Dictionary of National Biography, Tom & Tytler

British Gardens, Hadfield, Harlins, Highton (Publisher) A Zwemmer Ltd, London

The Potters Bar Zeppelin, J E Bennett

Occasional Papers of the Potters Bar & District Historical Society

Lines to Doncaster, Philip L Scowcroft, Doncaster Library

A Visitor's History of Hitchin, Anthony M Foster

Huntingdon Town Trail

Squire Waterton, Gilbert Phelps, E P Publishing Ltd

Wanderings in South America, Charles Waterton, T Nelson & Sons

Brassley's Battles, John Laffin

Byron, Frederick Raphael, Cardinal

Selected Poems and Prose of John Clare, Edited by Eric Robinson and Geoffrey Summerfield, Oxford University Press

The Life of John Clare, Frederick W Martin, 1964, London

The Buildings of England, Nikolaus Pevsner

The Kitchen Garden, David L Stuart, 1984, Hale

Ordnance Survey maps of the route

Woolsthorpe Manor, Colsterworth Newton's birthplace